How to use this book

Follow the advice, in italics, given for you on each page.

Support the children as they read the text that is shaded in cream.

***Praise** the children at every step!*

Detailed guidance is provided in the Read Write Inc. Phonics Handbook

9 reading activities

Children:

Practise reading the speed sounds.

Read the green, red and challenge words for the story.

Listen as you read the introduction.

Discuss the vocabulary check with you.

Read the story.

Re-read the story and discuss the 'questions to talk about'.

Read the story with fluency and expression.

Answer the questions to 'read and answer'.

Practise reading the speed words.

Speed sounds

Consonants *Say the pure sounds (do not add 'uh').*

f ff	l ll	m mm mb	n nn kn	r **rr**	s ss	v ve	z zz s	**sh**	th	ng nk

b bb	c k **ck**	d dd	g gg	h	j	p pp	qu	t **tt**	w wh	x	y	ch **tch**

Vowels *Say the sounds in and out of order.*

at	hen head	in	on	up	day	see happy	high find	blow no

zoo	look	car	for door snore	fair	whirl	shout	boy spoil

Each box contains one sound but sometimes more than one grapheme. Focus graphemes are ***circled****.*

Green words

Read in Fred Talk (pure sounds).

out test fresh cloth stop run catch fast fox

push pull clock head bread spread lead

Read in syllables.

hus`band → husband bott`om → bottom kitch`en → kitchen

craft`y → crafty cu`rrant → currant

Read the root word first and then with the ending.

finish → finished

lift → lifted

push → pushed

button → buttons

sing → singing

wink → winked

gasp → gasped

pull → pulled

stick → sticky

Red words

me to was her the said

you he of were they their

Challenge words

gingerbread oven

The gingerbread man

Introduction

Do you know what gingerbread men look like?
Imagine if they came alive.

Ann and Seth decided to cook some gingerbread men.
One of the gingerbread men decides he doesn't want to be eaten and he jumps off the tin and runs out of the kitchen.
They chase him. Others join in the chase.

Do you think they will catch him in the end?

Story written by Gill Munton
Illustrated by Tim Archbold

Vocabulary check

Discuss the meaning (as used in the story) after the children have read each word.

	definition:	sentence:
currants	*small black fruit like raisins*	*Ann put down the bag of currants.*
gasped	*breathed heavily, out of breath*	*'Stop!' gasped Seth.*
felt like lead	*really heavy*	*They ran so fast that their legs felt like lead.*
crafty	*clever*	*Then the crafty old fox began to run.*
dusty	*dirty, dry mud*	*The fox led him along a dusty track.*

Punctuation to note in this story:

1. Capital letters to start sentences and full stops to end sentences

2. Capital letters for names

3. Exclamation marks to show anger, shock and surprise

4. 'Wait and see' dots...

The gingerbread man

Hands, legs, a head ...

Six currants for buttons ...

and the last gingerbread man was finished!

Ann put down the bag of currants.

Her husband Seth pushed the tin of

gingerbread men into the hot oven.

That was when the last gingerbread man ... winked!

"I think I will get them out of the oven," said Seth at six o'clock.

He pulled the tin out, sniffed, and bit off a bit of leg.

"Well, I have got to test them," he said. "Mmmm! Fresh and crisp! Not bad!"

He left the tin next to the bread bin, with a cloth spread on top.

The last gingerbread man lifted his sticky head off the bottom of the tin.

He lifted the cloth. He lifted his legs – and jumped out!

He ran out of the kitchen!

"Stop!" yelled Seth.

"Stop!" yelled Ann.

He ran from Seth and Ann, singing,

"Run, run, as fast as you can!
You can't catch me.
I am the gingerbread man!"

Ann's black cat Lucky began to run as well.

"Stop!" yelled Seth.

"Stop!" yelled Ann.

"Stop!" yelled Lucky.

But the gingerbread man ran on.

"Run, run, as fast as you can!

You can't catch me. I am the gingerbread man!"

Seth's fat dog Bonzo began to run as well.

"Stop!" gasped Seth. "Stop!" gasped Ann.

"Stop!" gasped Lucky. "Stop!" gasped Bonzo.

They ran so fast that their legs felt like lead.

They had to stop to rest.

But the gingerbread man ran on.

"Run, run, as fast as you can!

You can't catch me.

I am the gingerbread man!"

Then the crafty old fox began to run.

"Stop!" he yelled. "Let me help you, gingerbread man!"

He licked his lips.

The gingerbread man stopped running

and grinned at the crafty old fox.

"Well, thanks!" he said.

The fox led him along a dusty track.

At the end of it was his den.

The crafty old fox licked his lips ...

and that was the end of the gingerbread man!

Questions to talk about

Re-read the page. Read the question to the children. Tell them whether it is a **FIND IT** *question or* **PROVE IT** *question.*

FIND IT

✓ *Turn to the page*

✓ *Read the question*

✓ *Find the answer*

PROVE IT

✓ *Turn to the page*

✓ *Read the question*

✓ *Find your evidence*

✓ *Explain why*

Page 9:	FIND IT	*What was odd about the last gingerbread man?*
Page 10:	FIND IT	*What did Seth do at six o'clock?*
Page 11:	PROVE IT	*Why do you think the gingerbread man ran away?*
Page 12:	PROVE IT	*How do Seth and Ann say 'Stop' to the gingerbread man? What type of voice do they use?*
Page 13:	PROVE IT	*Why were Ann, Seth, Bonzo and Lucky 'gasping' by now?*
Page 14:	PROVE IT	*Why does the writer describe the fox as 'crafty'?*
Page 15:	PROVE IT	*What happened to the gingerbread man at the end? Do you think it is a good ending?*

Questions to read and answer

(Children complete without your help.)

1. Seth got the gingerbread men out of the oven at **eleven o'clock / six o'clock / seven o'clock.**

2. Seth bit off the gingerbread man's **head / leg.**

3. Seth and Ann yelled **go / stop / hello.**

4. The fox led him to his **box / den / oven.**

5. The fox licked his **legs / head / lips.**

Speed words

Children practise reading the words across the rows, down the columns and in and out of order clearly and quickly.

out	fox	catch	fast	lifted
singing	head	bread	spread	lead
pulled	old	next	her	bottom
down	stop	sniff	husband	put